Frederick Douglass
Coloring Book

Gary Zaboly

Dover Publications
Garden City, New York

D1412268

Note

Frederick Douglass, an author, speaker, statesman, and activist for African Americans' civil rights, as well as women's rights, was born in Maryland in 1818 (some sources say 1817). A passionate abolitionist, Douglass experienced the injustices and brutality of slavery firsthand. He was born in his grandmother's slave cabin and worked in the field as a child, after having been separated from his mother (one of the practices of slavery). Although it was illegal to teach slaves to read and write, Douglass sought learning wherever he could, and eventually he became a public speaker, a newspaper publisher, and a writer. One of the highlights of his career occurred when he became an advisor to President Abraham Lincoln. Some of the quotations on these pages are taken from one of Douglass's three autobiographies, *Narrative of the Life of Frederick Douglass, an American Slave (1845)*.

Bibliographical Note

Frederick Douglass Coloring Book is a new work,
first published by Dover Publications in 2014.

International Standard Book Number

ISBN-13: 978-0-486-49215-5
ISBN-10: 0-486-49215-X

Manufactured in the United States of America
49215X04   2023
www.doverpublications.com

Frederick Douglass was born in 1818 in Tuckahoe, Talbot County, Maryland. According to custom, Frederick was separated from his mother at birth. He lived with his grandmother in her slave cabin. He would never learn the identity of his father. When he was only six years old, he began working in the field. His clothing was roughly made, and his food usually was coarse cornmeal mush.

At the age of eight, Frederick was sent to Baltimore to live with a new master, Hugh Auld. Living conditions there, for master and slave alike, were somewhat better than Frederick experienced in Tuckahoe. When he was twelve,

Mrs. Auld, whom Frederick called "Miss Sophia," began to teach him the alphabet. However, slaves were forbidden to learn how to read and write, and when Hugh Auld found out, he put an end to the lessons.

In 1833, sixteen-year-old Frederick was sent back to the Tuckahoe plantation, now run by Thomas Auld, Hugh's brother. Frederick was a smart and spirited lad, and Thomas Auld, wanting to "tame" him, gave Frederick, in his own words, "a number of severe whippings." When even these failed to tame the young man, Frederick was sent to live with Edward Covey, who was dubbed "the Negro Breaker . . . notorious for his fierce and savage disposition." Among Frederick's duties under the strict and watchful Covey were cutting wood and harvesting wheat, often in intense heat.

Covey's strong hand made Frederick at last feel broken, "in body, soul and spirit." When he was allowed some leisure time on Sundays, he would often go down to the nearby Chesapeake Bay shoreline and gaze at vessels sailing out to sea. "O, that I were free!" he mused. "O, that I were on one of your gallant decks, and under your protecting wing!"

Ever since learning the alphabet, Frederick had read, in secret, anything printed that he could get his hands on: the Bible, dictionaries, and school books, among others. Some of these were loaned to him by his young white friends, and others he purchased with what little money he earned from blacking the boots of gentlemen. In newspapers he learned about current events and life around the world, and he became especially interested in the growing abolitionist movement in the North.

Edward Covey's harsh treatment and frequent whip-lashing of Frederick became so intolerable that one day Frederick physically resisted him, "preventing him from injuring me, rather than trying to injure him." They grappled, but Frederick had grown into a very strong young man, and Covey was unable to break loose. After two hours Covey let go and drew away. "During the whole six months that I lived with Covey after this," wrote Frederick in his autobiography, "he never again laid the weight of his finger on me in anger."

In 1836, Frederick plotted to escape from his bondage with five fellow slaves. A canoe was to be stolen, which the fugitives planned to row to the head of Chesapeake Bay, and from there they would "bend our step toward the North-Star till we reached a free state." But one of the slaves betrayed the plot to their master. Armed constables were summoned, and they quickly confronted Frederick and his friend, John Harris. The two men were tied up and led to jail in the nearby town of Easton, Maryland.

"I was solitary and alone within the walls of a stone prison," Frederick would later write, "left to a fate of lifelong misery." His food allowance was "small and coarse," and sometimes slave traders would come by to examine him, on the chance that he would be available for purchase. Fortunately, his stay in jail lasted only a week, because his old master, Thomas Auld, arrived to bring him back to live again with his brother, Hugh Auld.

In 1837, Frederick fell in love with a resourceful free black woman named Anna Murray, who made a living in Baltimore as a laundress and housekeeper. Anna, a few years older than Frederick, encouraged him in his dream to escape slavery, promising to help him with clothes and money once he was ready.

On September 3, 1838, with the help of a few friends, including Anna Murray, Frederick finally escaped from his Baltimore captivity, boarding a northward-bound train dressed as a sailor. "My knowledge of ships and sailor's talk came much to my assistance," he wrote, "for I knew a ship from stem to stern, and from keelson to cross-trees, and could talk sailor like an 'old salt.'" He left the train at Wilmington, Delaware, and went by steamboat to Philadelphia, where he caught another train to New York. The entire journey from Maryland had taken less than a day.

In New York City, Frederick found lodging on Lispenard Street in the boarding house of abolitionist David Ruggles. The house was a station on the Underground Railroad, which helped escaped slaves travel to free northern cities, or to Canada. Frederick had already written to his intend-ed wife, Anna, to join him in New York. She "came at once on getting the good news of my safety," wrote Douglass, and they were married by the Reverend James W. C. Pennington, a black Presbyterian minister, in the presence of David Ruggles, on September 15, 1838.

Many bounty hunters from the South were in New York searching for fugitive slaves, so Frederick and Anna fled by ship to the seaport community of New Bedford, Massachusetts. In this antislavery town, blacks were employed in the whaling industry and related businesses. There Frederick took on the surname of Douglass, after a friend suggested that he use the name of one of the heroes in Sir Walter Scott's poem *The Lady of the Lake*. He made an income at various jobs. "I sawed wood," he wrote, "shoveled coal, dug cellars, moved rubbish from backyards, worked on the wharves, loaded and unloaded vessels, and scoured their cabins."

At a meeting of the Bristol Anti-Slavery Society in 1841, Douglass first heard abolitionist newspaper publisher William Lloyd Garrison speak. Eventually, the twenty-three-year-old Douglass was invited to tell his own story, and he thereafter continued to lecture on the evils of slavery—especially as viewed through his own experience—throughout the Northeast and Midwest.

While on an anti-slavery tour in Pendleton, Indiana, Frederick and his group were attacked by a mob. The speaking platform they had erected in the woods was torn down, and each abolitionist was beaten. Frederick tried to fight his way through the mob with a stick, but "they laid me prostrate on the ground," he recorded, "under a torrent of blows . . . in a state of unconsciousness." He was brought to the home of a Quaker family named Hardy, where his wounds were treated until he was able to walk again.

In 1845, *Narrative of the Life of Frederick Douglass: An American Slave* was published. Written entirely by Frederick himself, it fully and frankly told of his life as a slave, including the naming of his former owners. Douglass's friends, concerned that these men might try to capture Douglass, urged him to go to Great Britain until the publicity died down. Frederick set sail in August, finding himself "treated with every mark of respect from the beginning to the end of the voyage."

Douglass traveled throughout the United Kingdom, frequently lecturing and meeting many important people, from famous writers (including Hans Christian Andersen) to politicians and diplomats. He also spent much time in the company of English antislavery advocates, who eventually pooled their resources to buy Frederick's freedom from Thomas Auld for $700. In a letter he wrote to William Lloyd Garrison, Douglass noted that, in the United Kingdom, "I gaze around in vain for one who will question my equal humanity, claim me as a slave, or offer me an insult." Although urged by his new friends to remain in England, Frederick knew he had to return to America to continue the fight to free the three million blacks still in slavery there.

Frederick was back in the United States in the spring of 1847. During his time abroad he had become a nationwide celebrity, thanks to his bestselling *Narrative,* which had sold 5,000 copies during just the first four months of its release. From 1845 to 1849 the book went through six additional printings, and, by 1860, some 30,000 copies had been sold. The book also was translated and published in several European countries. Frederick would periodically revise its contents in editions published in 1855, 1881, and 1892. The book proved to be a major pillar of the antislavery movement.

Long inspired by William Lloyd Garrison's abolitionist newspaper, *The Liberator*, Douglass in 1847 moved to Rochester, New York, and published the first edition of his own vociferously antislavery paper, *The North Star*. Subscriptions came in very slowly, however, and he had to mortgage his home to keep the printing press going. Nevertheless, the paper enjoyed a run of twelve years. Douglass eventually printed other titles as well, including *Frederick Douglass Weekly*, *Frederick Douglass' Paper*, *Douglass' Monthly* and *New National Era*.

Frederick Douglass's Rochester home became a station on the Underground Railroad to nearby Canada. He often sheltered runaway slaves, once as many as eleven, until they were ready to move again. "I had some difficulty in providing so many with food and shelter," he wrote, "but, as may well be imagined, they were not very fastidious in either direction, and were well content with very plain food, and a strip of carpet on the floor for a bed, or a place on the straw in the barn loft."

Douglass was also an early supporter of the women's suf-fragist movement. He endorsed their right to vote at the first women's rights convention in 1848 at Seneca Falls, New York, where Elizabeth Cady Stanton also spoke. Realizing that Frederick Douglass was the perfect man from whom to gather firsthand knowledge about the lives of slaves in the South, novelist Harriet Beecher Stowe wrote to him (she had already consulted his *Narrative).*

Shortly after the 1852 publication of her huge bestseller, *Uncle Tom's Cabin,* she invited Douglass to visit her at her Andover, Massachusetts, home. There she solicited his advice as to what could be done to advance the lives of freed slaves in America. He advised her that it was most critical to form trade schools and workshops for young blacks, where they could learn employable skills.

Frederick Douglass had first met the abolitionist firebrand John Brown in 1847, and again eleven years later, when he invited Brown to stay in his Rochester house for several weeks. Brown was only months away from leading his raid on the Federal arsenal at Harpers Ferry, West Virginia, which he intended as the first blow in the violent liberation of the slaves. Although Douglass understood that it would probably take a war to free his black brethren, he did not believe that a slave insurrection would accomplish it, and therefore declined to get involved in Brown's plan.

In the early days of the Civil War, free northern blacks were employed not as soldiers in the Union army, but rather as laborers—ditch diggers, road and fort builders, teamsters, cooks, and so on. In his newspapers and elsewhere, Douglass strenuously advocated that blacks be allowed to serve in the Federal army. "I reproached the North that they fought the rebels with only one hand," he wrote, "when they might strike effectually with two."

Douglass and other abolitionists not only promoted the inclusion of black men in the Union army, but also, once this was finally approved by the government in 1862, helped enlist soldiers for the "colored" regiments. The most famous of these regiments was the 54th Massachusetts (although many volunteers came from other states). Two of Douglass's sons, Charles and Lewis, served in its ranks. As ordered by law, the officers were to be white men; the colonel was twenty-five-year-old Robert Gould Shaw, who had been born into an abolitionist Boston family.

Black soldiers throughout the war proved their mettle on the battlefield, winning the respect of their fellow soldiers and northern citizens alike. One of their most famous actions was the July 18, 1863, assault on the Confederate fort Battery Wagner, which guarded the sea approach to Charleston, South Carolina. In concert with other Union units, the 54th Regiment attacked under a terrific barrage of cannon and small arms fire, and although they passed the ditch and climbed the parapets to engage the defenders, the 54th was eventually beaten back with a total loss of killed (including Colonel Shaw), wounded, and missing of 272 men. Sergeant-Major Lewis Douglass had been in the thick of the action and was wounded by a canister shot. By the end of the war, almost one-tenth of the Union Army was composed of black soldiers.

To Douglass's great joy, the Emancipation Proclamation was passed in January 1863. Even though more than two years of war remained to be fought, the proclamation declared that all enslaved people in the South were now free. Douglass first met President Lincoln in July of 1863, at the White House. It was the first of many meetings. "I was never more quickly or more completely put at ease in the presence of a great man than in that of Abraham Lincoln," he wrote. The purpose of Douglass's visit was, among other things, to request that black soldiers receive the same wages as whites, to assure them the same protection if taken prisoner, and to include them in prisoner exchanges. Lincoln promised to do what he could on each request.

After the war, Douglass continued to lecture, championing voting rights for the freed blacks as well as the 1870 passage of the Fifteenth Amendment, which prohibited the state and Federal governments from denying American citizens of any race or color the right to vote. Two years later, he became the first African American nominated for Vice President, on the Equal Rights Party ticket, with suffragist Victoria Woodhull as its presidential candidate— the first woman to run for that office (President Ulysses S. Grant was easily elected to a second term that November). In 1872, Douglass lost nearly all of his personal papers when his house caught fire; arson was suspected.

In 1878, Douglass returned to the old Maryland plantation that he had not seen since his slave days, and he visited with his former master, the now aged and dying Thomas Auld. "We shook hands cordially," wrote Frederick, "and in the act of doing so, he, having been long stricken with palsy, shed tears as men thus afflicted will do when excited by any deep emotion . . . his condition affected me deeply, and for a time choked my voice and made me speechless." The forgiveness Douglass expressed was cathartic for both men, although Auld did not long survive after this last visit with his former slave. Frederick never forgot what Auld told him: "I always knew you were too smart to be a slave, and had I been in your place, I should have done as you did."

In 1879, President Rutherford B. Hayes named Frederick Douglass the United States Marshal for the District of Columbia. In 1881, he was named Recorder of Deeds for Washington, D.C., by President Garfield, and he remained in that position for five years. Douglass continued to help raise money for thousands of ex-slaves moving north. In 1884, two years after the death of his beloved Anna, he married Helen Pitts, a white woman who was a feminist and the daughter of an abolitionist. Their marriage sparked predictable outrage in many circles, but they stayed together happily until his death eleven years later.

On rare occasions, Douglass found time for leisure. He was an accomplished violinist and enjoyed attending classical music concerts. He also noted, during the course of a life full of incredible challenges, that "I have been greatly helped to bear up under unfriendly conditions, too, by a constitutional tendency to see the funny side of things." In 1886 and 1887 he and Helen toured England, France, Italy, Egypt, and Greece. At the age of seventy, Frederick managed to climb to the top of the highest pyramid near Cairo. "Neither in ascending nor descending is it safe to look down," he wrote. "One misstep and all is over . . . While nothing could tempt me to climb the rugged, jagged, steep and perilous sides of the Great Pyramid again, yet I am very glad to have had the experience once, and once is enough for a lifetime."

In 1889, Douglass was appointed U.S. Minister to Haiti by President Benjamin Harrison, a post he stayed with for two years. In 1892, he helped construct affordable rental homes for blacks in Baltimore. Following a speech he gave at a meeting of the National Council of Women in Washington D.C., on February 20, 1895, seventy-seven-year-old Douglass died of either a heart attack or a stroke. The monuments to him are many, and some of them are shown above. Starting clockwise at the upper right are: a statue erected at the northwest corner of New York's Central Park; the Frederick Douglass home at Cedar Hill, Washington D.C., where he lived from 1878 until his death, and now a National Historic Site; the Frederick Douglass Monument in Highland Park, Rochester, New York; the Frederick Douglass Memorial Park, Staten Island, New York; and the grave of Frederick Douglass in Mount Hope Cemetery, Rochester, New York.